SERVING
YOUR
GENERATION
BY
UNDERSTANDING
ASSIGNMENT

Serving Your Generation by Understanding Assignment
ISBN-13:
978-1722037062

ISBN-10:
1722037067

Published by
Ashley Estrada Ministries
Kissimmee, FL
www.ashleyestradaministries.com

DEDICATION

I dedicate this book to Our Lord Jesus Christ, who considered me faithful by putting me in the ministry, and who liberated me from the opinions of men, thus equipping me to serve my generation.

To my wife, Marcia Judith Estrada, the greatest source of my inspiration and the one who encouraged me to put this book in print. She is the one who has shared me with the world for the past thirty-eight years. I thank you, Honey, for sticking with me through all of my transitions.

To all my children, Joel, Kenneth, Kristel, Jesse and Jeriah, you too have also shared me with the rest of the world. Although I could not be home on a constant basis, because of my travels, you have remained faithful to the Lord. This is much more than a father could ask for.

A special dedication goes to Kenneth, who has brought great joy to my heart in answering the call to serve your generation. I know that you will accomplish much more than I ever will.

To the saints and leadership of Kingdom Life International, St. Thomas, under the pastoral leadership of Bernaby and Deborah Joseph, I dedicate this book. It would have been extremely difficult for me to have answered the call to the world, without your faithful support.

Finally, to two great men of God who had a tremendous impact on my life and who influenced me to become who I am today, I dedicate this book to you: the late Apostle Clifford E Turner of Liberty Temple, Chicago, IL. and Rev. Jefferson Edwards of Kansas City, Missouri.

CONTENTS

ACKNOWLEDGEMENTS

I would like to acknowledge the many individuals who helped in one way or another in the birthing of this book.

Thanks to the many of God's prophets and prophetesses who over the years have prophesied to me about the releasing of the books that were within me. I always knew that they were there but lacked the discipline to put it to paper.

Thanks to my wife, Marcia for the painstaking job of editing and typing the manuscript.

Thanks to my son, Pastor Kenneth Estrada, who despite his own busy schedule, designed and did the layout of this book and took care of all the details needed to get it published.

To Joan Morain, who worked with AEM and who stayed on my case to finish this book, along with all the supporters and partners of AEM, thank you.

To all my spiritual and adopted sons and daughters in the Lord, thank you for allowing me to speak into your lives and for making my assignment a joyful and productive one.

I also want to acknowledge the role of the first pastors I ever had who gave me the opportunity to answer the call of God upon my life by helping to facilitate the cost of my Bible College education, Pastors Don and Janice Scheske.

To a band of brothers who got saved around the same time with me, attended Bible School together and are still involved in the ministry today, I salute you all: Gilbert Cuffy, Oliver Jackson, Peter Piper and Hubert Lazarus Murray.

To my dear friend, Bishop Garvin Garraway, a man who is true to His word and one of the greatest examples that I have seen when it comes to giving, I acknowledge you and the inspiration that you have been to me. Even though you constantly say that you learned it from me, you have exceeded me in this gift. Finally, to all those who have played a very important part in helping me to get to where I am today, I thank you all. Many of you have been major pieces of the puzzle to my life and you shall receive your reward, even if I have not been able to name all of you.

FOREWORD

Ashley Estrada began his spiritual journey during the missionary ministry of my wife and me in the island Commonwealth of Dominica in 1974. Ashley, a young civil engineering assistant was a typical young man taken up with the lifestyle of a free and unrestrained culture. God had other plans for him! One day, in God's providence, he walked by a street service where he received Christ into his life. He grew rapidly in his newfound freedom in Jesus. He consumed the Word and showed every sign that God had destined him for great things.   During those years God lead us to train and mobilize many young men and women to evangelize on the street corners of the cities, towns and villages thought the island.   Ashley was one of those street preachers who honed his skills in preaching with great power and authority and soon became one of our finest and successful evangelists.

God has called you and me to be the facilitators of the "Call of God." We enabled Ashley in those early years sending him to seminary to be equipped and grounded in the Word of God.   His ministry, beginning in Dominica, then to St. Thomas USVI, and has now spread to the entire world.   Who could have imagined what God would do through this humble and dedicated servant?   We have followed with great joy the ministry of Ashley and are privileged to have had a "Paul – Timothy" relationship in his ministry formation years.

This book accurately describes the historically proven principles of preparation, transformation and empowerment that have accompanied every God-initiated outpouring of His Holy Spirit. I sincerely believe that the twelve principles that Evangelist Ashley Estrada shares in this book, when implemented, will revolutionize your effectiveness in life and ministry.

Donald E Scheske
Indianapolis, Indiana

"SERVING YOUR GENERATION" is a must have tool for everyone who desires to fulfill the destiny that is unique to them alone. We all have been created to complete an assignment for the generation in which we have been born, and it is easy to allow life, people and circumstances to circumvent our God ordained path. In this book, Apostle Ashley Estrada clearly and concisely lays out the earmarks of divine assignment. You will understand how to ascertain, obtain and remain in God's unique and infallible plan for your life. Particularly those who have radical and vanguard assignments, "SERVING YOUR GENERATION" is an arsenal of foundational principles and timeless insight, to unapologetically fulfill your purpose and destiny. As one who witnessed such a call, as lived out in the life of my late husband, Chief Apostle Clifford E. Turner, who indeed served his generation well with boldness, power, and integrity, I can attest to the accuracy and the potency of applying the criterion outlined in this book.

Elect Lady Darlyn C. Turner
President
The Liberty International Network

INTRODUCTION

This book has been long overdue. I have shared with leaders in many nations the principles that I am about to share in this book.

It was while speaking at a conference of pastors in the nation of the Kingdom of Cambodia in 2017, that my wife Marcia, who was watching the conference on Facebook Live, encouraged me to put it in print. I believe that as you read this book, God will birth within you a great desire to serve your generation.

There are too many unmarked graves in cemeteries around the world. There are others with headstones, but their names are unknown. It is not how long we live on the earth but how impactful our lives are while we are alive. Each of us should seek to leave our mark on the earth so that it will be said of us, that we continue to speak even though we have died. (Hebrews 11:4). This happens only when we decide to serve our generation by the will of God. Our attitude must be that we refuse to die until we have served our generation.

Will we have a report like this? "For David, after he had served his own generation by the will of God, fell on sleep, and was laid unto his fathers, and saw corruption:" (Acts 13:36)

In this book, I am going to share twelve principles which I believe will help you, even as they have been helping me. I am convinced that as we allow these principles to govern our lives, especially those of us who are in positions of leadership, we can come to the end of our assignment here on earth totally fulfilled. The Apostle Paul, came to the end of his life knowing that he had served his generation by the will of God. Facing certain death, he triumphantly proclaimed, "I have fought a good fight, I have finished my course, I have kept the faith" (2 Timothy 4:7)

WHY IS DAVID REGARDED AS ISRAEL'S MOST
BELOVED AND SUCCESSFUL KING?
WHY DID GOD, DESPITE DAVID'S FAULTS, CALL
HIM A MAN AFTER HIS OWN HEART?

IT WAS BECAUSE DAVID UNDERSTOOD THAT
HIS ASSIGMENT WAS TO
SERVE HIS GENERATION

CHAPTER
01

THE ROLE OF ASSIGNMENT

The Bible tells us in Acts 13:36 *For David, after he had served his own generation by the will of God, fell on sleep, and was laid unto his fathers, and saw corruption.*

Why is David regarded as Israel's most beloved and successful king? Why did God, despite David's faults, call him a man after His own heart? It was because David understood that his assignment was to serve his generation.

It is important that we, too, understand that our

assignment is to serve our generation. We are not responsible for the mistakes of the past generation. We must focus on serving our present generation. In doing so, we will help to mold future generations.

Generational Impact

David had such an impact on his generation, that God, Himself, adopted the system of worship that David instituted and decided that it would be the model that His church would adopt. In Acts 15:16-18, the apostle, James, refers to the restoration of the Tabernacle of David:

16 "'After this I will return and rebuild David's fallen tent. Its ruins I will rebuild, and I will restore it,
17 that the rest of mankind may seek the Lord, even all the Gentiles who bear my name, says the Lord, who does these things'
18 things known from long ago.
-Acts 15:16-18 (NIV)

As great a leader as Moses was in leading the children of Israel and introducing them to the God of their fathers, God did not choose to restore the Tabernacle of Moses. In fact, it passed away.

David's impact upon his generation, caused God to promise David an eternal lineage.

*For this is what the LORD says: 'David will never fail
to have a man to sit on the throne of Israel,*
-Jeremiah 33:17 (HCSB)

*When your days are complete and you lie down with
your fathers, I will raise up your descendant after you,
who will come forth from you, and I will establish his
kingdom. He shall build a house for My name, and I
will establish the throne of his kingdom forever.*
-2 Samuel 7:12-13 (NASB)

This of course will be fulfilled in Jesus, as the Son of David, who will set up His everlasting kingdom in the earth.

David introduced the children of Israel to a new form of worship which they had never seen before. In the Tabernacle of Moses, the people only saw God as a fearful, unapproachable Being. Their worship was based more on fear than on joy. David was the one who introduced the children of Israel to the aspect of praise, accompanied by joy in their worship of God.

David had such a revelation of that aspect of worship and what it meant to God that he employed singers and musicians in shifts, to sing and offer praise to God continuously. Even though David lived for only seventy years, what he accomplished in those short years, caused God to make an eternal promise to him, that his system of worship would never die. He is an example of one being dead but continuing to speak.

He lived for his generation. He was focused on serving his generation.

We, too, must become focused on serving our generation. So how do we go about doing that?

The Nature of Assignment

The first thing we must understand is the nature of assignment. We need to understand that our lives consist of various assignments and that everyone does not have the same assignment. The more quickly we come to that realization, is the more quickly we will discover how we can serve our generation. We have heard it said many times, "You were created an original, don't die as a copy". If you want to make a lasting impact, you have to allow God to utilize what makes you uniquely you and to fashion it for His purpose.

PEOPLE DESIROUS OF
SERVING THEIR GENERATION
CANNOT ALLOW OTHERS TO PUT UNDUE PRESSURE
UPON THEM.

YOU MUST KNOW YOUR ASSIGNMENT
AND YOU MUST REALIZE THAT

GOD IS ALWAYS GOING TO OPERATE ACCORDING TO HIS TIMETABLE, NOT YOURS, AND NOT THAT OF OTHER PEOPLE

CHAPTER
02

Principle #1
YOU CANNOT OPERATE UNDER PRESSURE

I will forever be grateful to one of the early mentors in ministry, Apostle Jefferson Edwards, who was used by God to help me understand this principle. Before Jeff came into my life, I was a very timid preacher always concerned about people's opinion about me. I was so intimidated by others that I could not look them in the eye when speaking to them. The Lord used Jeff to release such a radical anointing upon my life, that the person I am today, is worlds apart from the person I was before.

What do we mean when we say that you cannot

operate under pressure? We mean that people desirous of serving their generation cannot allow others to put undue pressure upon them. You must know your assignment and you must realize that God is always going to operate according to His timetable, not yours, and not that of other people.

Timing and Leading

People tend to want you to operate within their timeframe. Jesus' brothers wanted Him to operate in their timeframe. (John 7:2-6). They wanted to know why he was not going to the Feast of Tabernacles.

John 7:2-6 (NIV)

2 But when the Jewish Festival of Tabernacles was near, 3 Jesus' brothers said to him, "Leave Galilee and go to Judea, so that your disciples there may see the works you do. 4 No one who wants to become a public figure acts in secret. Since you are doing these things, show yourself to the world." 5 For even his own brothers did not believe in him.

6 Therefore Jesus told them, "My time is not yet here; for you any time will do.

This is a clear case of family members trying to pressure Him to perform or produce before His time. It happens to all of us. But it's more difficult to resist it when those seeking to press us into what they perceive is our destiny, are family and friends, whom we believe have our best interests at heart.

Jesus resisted the pressure that his brothers were applying.

We must know and be convinced of the leading *and* timing of God as it relates to our assignment.

However, we need balance here. Many people use the excuse that they are praying and waiting for the Lord to tell them when to move. They use this as a cover up for their laziness or fear of taking risks. That's not what I'm dealing with here. I'm dealing with individuals who are like stallions, ready for the race track, but are being restrained in the paddock. They are burning with vision inside but know that they cannot allow the pressure from others to cause them to bolt and break open the door. They do whatever needs to be done while waiting for the green light from the Father. The green light might not come on suddenly. The Lord might just ease us into it. But we must stay open to His Spirit and allow Him to lead us.

The Will of God Shouldn't Frustrate You

I am convinced that the will of God is not supposed to frustrate His people. Why should the will of God be a frustrating thing? *"For it is God who works in you to will and to act in order to fulfill his good purpose". Philippians 2:13 (NIV)* I believe that the will of God should bring peace to the child of God. It is not a mystical thing. It is not a "spooky" thing. Too many believers think that knowing God's will involves a great struggle. They spend a lot of time waiting for the will of God. Some wait for a word from a prophet or prophetess to reveal the will of God for their lives. They do not know that in most cases, the word of prophecy should simply confirm or expand what they should already have sensed in their spirits.

I remember during my earlier years of ministry, on two separate occasions, I was offered a large congregation. They were very tempting offers. To accept them would have brought money, prestige and a fast-track to "success" according to how people tend to rate success. But both times I knew that it was not the will of God for my life. However, only in one instance did I receive a prophetic word which confirmed what I already sensed in my spirit. This is how it happened.

We had recently relocated from our first pastorate. Like Abraham, we had left in obedience to God, but not knowing where our next assignment would be. We had two pre-school children and no stable income. It had been a move of faith.

While in this state of transition, our family began fellowshipping at a church and became friends with the pastor. He invited me to preach a few times. One Sunday morning, to our dismay, the pastor was forced to resign, not for any wrong-doing but because of a board that was very controlling. My wife and I decided that we could not continue fellowshipping there and so did not return.

One Sunday morning, I was preaching at another church, when a dear woman of God approached me at the end of the service and told me that the Lord had awakened her that morning with a message for me. He had told her to tell me that an offer was going to be made to me which would appear very lucrative, but if accepted, would spell the death of my ministry. At the time, I knew of no such offer and told her so. However, I kept the word in my heart. A few days after, one of the board members of that church came to me and told me that the board had been wanting to get in touch with me. Thankfully, in my own spirit, I knew that I would not accept any offer to be the pastor of that church, and additionally, God had reinforced my decision by sending His word through one of his handmaidens.

The second instance took place under different circumstances. We already had a thriving church, which we had founded. I began to travel out of the United States to another country very frequently. I felt loved and appreciated by those people and after some time, one of the ministers there offered me the opportunity to pastor one of their churches. They would give me a house, a luxurious car, and a great salary. But in my spirit, I did not have a peace about it and so I thanked him but refused his offer.

Know His Will

This is what I practice as it relates to knowing the will of God for my life. First, I understand that the will of God should not frustrate me. Secondly, I say to the Lord that I am open to Him to lead me into whatever He has for me and that I will not rush ahead of Him and try to make things happen in the flesh. Thirdly, I let Him know that I will be obedient to Him and I will relax in Him until He makes it clear to me.

This does not mean that I adopt a passive state of mind. I know that what I want to do and accomplish, is not half done and so I cannot give up. There is a drive inside of me that is seeking to find expression to serve my generation. Therefore, I anticipate each day with the thought, "Could this be the day, that what the Lord has spoken over my life and what I know in my spirit, will begin to come into greater manifestation?"

So, there is always great expectation in my spirit. I refuse to be frustrated. I'm not here to allow people to put any pressure upon me. You should not allow it either. Too many believers are allowing other people to try to live their lives through them and end up living under condemnation and guilt. We shall look at that in more detail in a later chapter. For the moment, just remember that understanding the will of God for your life is crucial to serving your generation.

BE CAREFUL WHO OR WHAT
YOU ALLOW TO DEFINE YOU...

...WHOMEVER OR WHATEVER
YOU ALLOW TO
DEFINE YOU WILL CONFINE YOU

CHAPTER
03

Principle #2
BE A REFORMER NOT A CONFORMER

When we hear that someone is not a conformer, we tend to think that he or she is a rebel.

In this context however, we are talking about those who refuse to conform to the mold that was created for them by the world system or religious systems. They cannot be bought. They do not belong to people or systems. They are not seeking to win a popularity contest. They are radical. They are not concerned about the accolades of, nor titles given to them, but let their office or assignment speak for them. They are consumed by their burning passion to serve their generation.

Title or Assignment?

I find it very disheartening to see that in the Kingdom of God today, people seem to be more concerned about titles than about assignment. I heard of an incident in which the secretary of a church, called another church and asked to speak with the pastor of that church. When the pastor came on the line, and she addressed him as "pastor", he immediately corrected her and said, "excuse me, it's apostle".

Occurrences like this cause me to wonder whether even those of us who walk in the five-fold ministry, understand that our principal assignment is to serve our generation.

There are so many other stories that I can tell here about similar situations, but I choose to focus on the positive. Let me point out that those who are consumed with the passion of serving their generation are not "religious" people.

Did you raise your eyebrows when you read that statement? Aren't Christian people, religious people? When I say that those who want to serve their generation are not religious people, I'm referring to the fact that even though these people may belong to a denomination, or movement, they do not allow themselves to be defined by that.

Defined.... Confined!

I often make this statement in many of my messages, "Be careful who or what you allow to define you, because whomever or whatever you allow to define you, will CONFINE you". This is something we all need to think seriously about.

I refuse to allow religion to define me. Because I travel quite a lot, whenever I'm returning to the United States, I'm asked many times what is my religion? I chafe when I'm asked that. There are times that I say that I have no religion, but because I know what they mean, I concede by saying that I believe in the "full gospel". When I must complete forms that require me to state my occupation, I refuse to put "minister of religion" because I am neither a minister of or for religion.

I have also been told on several occasions, that I don't look like a pastor. But what is a pastor supposed to look like? Whatever that is, apparently, I did not seem to fit the mold that most people attributed to a "pastoral" demeanor or appearance.

When you allow your denomination or religious affiliation to define you, be prepared to be confined by it. You are going to have to toe the line. Then what are you going to do if they do not operate by or believe in Kingdom principles?

If you serve Jesus and know Him as your Lord and Savior, you know that He was not a CONFORMER, but a REFORMER and TRANSFORMER.

He was compassionate and merciful, but He was also confrontational when He needed to be.

I'm not proposing that we go about trying to oppose everything and looking for arguments to debate. Personally, I avoid arguments and debates. I am so focused on my assignment that I have no time for that. I refuse to serve religion. I refuse to allow people to create a mold for me. I am not concerned with their titles. My concern is how can I better serve my generation.

I encourage you too, to examine what or who might be trying to define you and to honestly answer the question, are you free from influences that might be vying for control of your destiny? Is there a conflict between what the Lord is impressing upon your spirit and what your organization or denomination is expecting of you? Always keep in mind the words of Jesus, "No man can serve two masters". You cannot serve God and money at the same time, but neither can you serve God and the religion of man.

ALLOW THE STORIES OF OTHERS TO MOTIVATE
YOU, BUT DO NOT TRY TO COPY THEM. WHAT
WORKED FOR THEM MAY NOT WORK FOR YOU.

STUDY THEIR PRINCIPLES AND DISCIPLINES,
BUT ALWAYS REMEMBER THAT YOU ARE UNIQUE.
YOU ARE NOT A DUPLICATE,
YOU ARE AN ORIGINAL

CHAPTER 04

Principle #3
DO NOT LIVE ACCORDING TO PEOPLE'S UNREASONABLE EXPECTATIONS

Before we proceed I need to stress on the word "unreasonable". People who have mentored us, made investments in our lives, and stood with us, usually have high expectations of us because they want to see us succeed. But there are others who try to place undue pressure on us based on their expectations, which are oftentimes unreasonable.

Those of us who are mature and have attained some measure of success, need to be careful that we do not interpret what others are doing in the light of our own success. Just because we may have gotten quickly to where we are, does not mean that others can get there at the same pace as we did. Therefore, let us not put undue pressure on them to meet our expectations.

I want to also address those of you who have the tendency to look at the "success" of others and to feel the pressure to live up to some of the expectations that you think are required of you. You must become aware of these self-imposed destructive expectations and remove them from your life.

Allow the stories of others to motivate you, but do not try to copy them. What worked for them may not work for you. Yes, study their principles and disciplines but always remember that you are unique. You are not a duplicate, you are an original.

Staying with Your Assignment

It will help you to know that there are individuals who have missed it as far as their assignment was concerned. Consciously or unconsciously, they try to place unreasonable expectations on others to compensate for what they see as lost opportunity.

It is dangerous to miss our assignment in life. When we do, it means that the effect that we should have had on our generation, will be minimal. It is dangerous to miss your assignment. You can begin to be jealous of others who are experiencing success because they are staying with their assignment.

I know of a great servant of the Lord, whom the Lord had positioned to be a mighty voice in his nation. It was almost as though the Lord had placed that nation in the palms of His servant. Just when things were about to open in that nation, he left with his family. Many prominent men and women of God were disappointed. Some even cautioned him because they knew that he was abandoning his assignment. It was to no avail. His mind was made up. That man of God never experienced any significant success after that. Churches he tried to establish never amounted to much and are not even in existence today.

Do not allow people to push you to show yourself to the world if you know that you are not ready.

Be full of dreams and visions but know how to discern when it is your vision and not someone else's unreasonable expectations being imposed upon you.

In 2010, after thirty-one years of full time pastoral work, I turned that aspect of the ministry over to one of my spiritual sons. I know what it is like to have unreasonable expectations placed upon me. During those years of being a pastor, I met many wonderful people. I loved them dearly. But there were always some who believed that they knew what I should do better than I knew myself. There were those who expected me to do things a certain way and who got offended when I would not. I am not saying that I was beyond taking advice and suggestions from my congregation. I am saying that I had to know what God had called ME to do.

What About Your Church?

If you are a pastor, don't try to be like any other pastor. Don't seek to make the church that you lead become like any other church. In Revelation, when Jesus addressed the seven churches, he had a commendation for each of them as well as a rebuke. His rebuke was never a result of their failure to do what another church was doing, but because they had not embraced their assignment.

What about your church? Are you just another church in your area or is there something unique about you? For what purpose does your church exist? Is it a voice in your community that is distinct from those around you? Or are you putting your people under undue pressure because you are trying to be like someone else?

It was so refreshing to me when I visited Hartland Church in Indianapolis, Indiana. The pastor of the church is Darryn Scheske, the son of Don and Janice Scheske who were my first pastors and mentors back in 1974. Darryn and his wife had started the ministry which has grown phenomenally but they had employed such a unique approach that I felt I had to hear Darryn's story.

My wife always says that I ask too many questions. To which I reply that it's in so doing that I get to know people and can better understand them and relate to them. For if you don't know where someone came from, how will you be able to relate to where they are and where they are going?

So, as I was being given a tour of the ministry and its facilities, I utilized the opportunity to ask as many questions as I could. I must confess, I was awestruck. I had not seen him in over thirty years. He was three years old the last time I saw him. Yet here he was, so obviously serving his generation. I had no doubt that he had discovered his assignment. He's not puffed up, has a genuine love and desire to help others, does not operate under pressure, and is not trying to live up to people's expectations.

David and Michal

I remember the story of David recounted in 2 Samuel 6:14, when he successfully brought the ark back to Jerusalem. He was so ecstatic that the ark had returned to its rightful place, that he danced with all his might before the Lord. **David was not concerned about what people thought about him. He knew what the ark signified to his nation. He knew that the presence of the God of Israel had returned to God's people.** But when Michal, David's wife, and Saul's daughter, looked down and saw King David leaping and dancing before the Lord, the Bible says that she despised him in her heart.

God accepted David's dance of praise, but Michal felt that it was inappropriate for him, a king, to behave like that publicly. She acted upon her own unreasonable expectations of him and proceeded to upbraid him. She quenched his joy when he returned to bless his household after having blessed the congregation.

Although this is not a marriage manual, if your spouse is seeking to serve his or her generation, do not try to impose your unreasonable expectations on him or her, or be one who quenches his or her passion. A strong person can endure much of the attacks that come from outside, but when that person arrives at home, there should be a balm waiting to be applied to the hurts and wounds.

I am so grateful to the wife that the Lord gave me since 1979. I have had some storms in my lifetime. I have been betrayed and misunderstood. But I always knew that there was someone with the balm, at home. She never kills my dreams, my vision, or my joy. She knows how to stoke the fire that's within me that's propelling me to the understanding of my assignment.

Therefore, be very careful of standing in the way of someone who is intent on serving their generation. God takes seriously the assignments that He gives His servants. If you doubt me, look at Michal, she remained barren until the day of her death. David in his defense of his refusal to give in to her unreasonable expectations, said in **2 Samuel 6:21-22**

> *21 So David said to Michal, "It was before the LORD, who chose me instead of your father and all his house, to appoint me ruler over the people of the LORD, over Israel. Therefore I will play music before the LORD.*
> *22 And I will be even more undignified than this, and will be humble in my own sight. (NKJV)*

I distinctly remember a period in my life when the Lord was processing me for one of the assignments in my life. In order to use me effectively, God had to break a spirit of intimidation off of my life. He Himself placed a radical anointing upon my life to the extent that some of my pastoral staff became concerned and wanted me to "tone things down a bit". I'm sure they meant well, but in my heart, I knew that God was doing a deep work in my life. As much as I respected them, I could not back down and give in to their expectations as to how a senior pastor, should dress, or behave. I did not let the community dictate what I should drive or where I should live.

It was tough, and I was accused of a lot of things. But looking back, I'm so thankful that I did not give in to their expectations or that of the community to which I had been sent. I have mellowed quite a bit now, but it was necessary for me to go through that transformation in my life at that point in time, for it had everything to do with part of my assignment to serve my generation.

For the People

Today, I can help other younger ministers who are struggling to discover their assignment. I carry within me a great burden for young ministers. Hence the reason that as far back as 1991, our ministry has sponsored Leadership conferences with the intent to expose younger ministers to what the Lord is doing in their generation. Through these conferences, many of them got a bigger picture of what their assignment was all about. They received the confirmation that the Hand of the Lord was upon their lives, not for the ordinary, but for the extraordinary.

I have tried many times to move away from having these conferences, but I am always pulled back to them. I am convinced that this is part of the mandate that is upon my life.

As you may perhaps be struggling to break free from others' expectations of you, let me leave you with this nugget.

Jesus never gave Himself *to* the people but *for* the people.

When I admonished the pastors at a conference in Cambodia that they must never give themselves to the people but for the people, a pastor who oversees about seven to eight hundred churches, was very disturbed and came to me to inquire further. I explained to him that when you give yourself TO the people, you relinquish control of your life to them, but when you give yourself FOR the people, you can serve them while allowing only the Holy Spirit of God to be in control. As his understanding was enlightened, a big smile came over that overseer's face and I believe he can now empower other pastors with this understanding also.

Love people, care for them deeply, but never give yourself to them. Also, be wary of those who give gifts to you with the intention of manipulating you. Many people genuinely love their leaders and wish to bless them with material things as the scriptures admonish. However, leaders must learn to discern genuine givers from those who have ulterior motives and those who want to impose their expectations on you. Believe the best about everyone but always remember that you are dealing with man. People's attitudes towards you can change without warning and then they will turn around and reproach you because of the gifts that they gave when they loved you.

Here is another nugget of wisdom that leaders who want to be free from the demands of others' expectations, will do well to follow. Do not borrow money from members of your congregation. When you borrow money from a member, you become their servant. Hear the advice of Solomon from *Proverbs 22:7 "The rich rules over the poor and the borrower is servant to the lender" (NKJV).* When you borrow, it leads to bondage. You put yourself in a position where you must watch your words with that individual. You may compromise your ability to correct him or her. That is why, early in our ministry, my wife and I decided never to borrow money from the members we pastored over the years. If we didn't have it, we prayed and believed God to come through for us.

So, shake off the yoke of people's unreasonable expectation of you and be free to serve your generation.

GET YOUR OWN SWAG,
CREATE YOUR OWN QUOTE,
PRODUCE YOUR OWN MUSIC....
YOU HAVE DANCED LONG
ENOUGH TO OTHERS' MUSIC,
NOW IT'S THEIR TURN TO DANCE TO YOURS

CHAPTER 05

Principle #4
DON'T DANCE TO PEOPLE'S MUSIC....
CREATE YOUR OWN

What do I mean by not dancing to people's music? Does that not sound egoistic or prideful? No, this is not the intention here. We are talking about becoming an innovator, a trendsetter, a trailblazer, a leader, a voice and not an echo, an original and not a duplicate.

Too many people do not want to make the necessary sacrifices. They only want to piggy back on the backs of others who have spent time, energy and resources to be where they are today. Yes, we all can benefit from the work of others. We do not need to reinvent the proverbial wheel, but at the same time we must be willing to be creative. It is time for us to dance to our own tunes and to stop being like the children of Hamlin, who danced to the music of the Pied Piper, to their demise.

I have seen people in leadership who never take the time to hear from God themselves. They never take the time to study the Word for themselves but prefer to preach another's revelation. God has something that He wants to reveal to them but they cannot hear because they are so insecure that they resort to sermon outlines from books, another preacher or those they hear on television.

I know that there are ministers who encourage us to preach their messages, with the admonition to be sure to "copy it right". I also understand that in the process of listening to a speaker, sometimes one statement they make, may ignite a new thought and give birth to a message or revelation in us. This has happened to me on many occasions. Nothing is wrong with that. That is perfectly normal. But if week after week, we have no insight or revelation of our own, and must resort to regurgitate another's message, we must seriously question whether we are functioning in the right place.

Song writers and musicians spend time to produce original songs and music. The inspiration might come suddenly but it takes hard work and discipline to produce the final version. They work long hours at the studio to ensure that their work is perfect. Do you realize that it is the artist that produces the originals that earns the royalties? Even after they die, every time someone uses their music or song, their estate collects royalties.

My desire for you is that you learn to "write your own song" and "dance to your own music".

Don't wait for someone else to create the music for you because the melody is in your heart.

If you take time to work on it, to develop it and to add your own flair to it, the Lord will use you to bless others. But it's going to take discipline. I wrote most of this book on long, intercontinental flights. Honestly, I wanted so much to just relax and watch movies. But I realized that if I'm going to create my own music, I must be disciplined, forget about watching movies and focus on my writing.

It's been many years since so many prophetic words were spoken over my life about the books that were inside of me that needed to come out. I knew that those were accurate prophecies, but I never had the drive to stop and concentrate on getting them on paper. Do you know what I discovered? I found out that once you discipline yourself and start, the inspiration comes. Before this book was even completed, I was already looking forward to writing the other books.

Those of us who are intent on serving our generation must create our own music. We cannot be effective if we continue to dance all the time to somebody else's music. However, let's not get off balance and think that if something did not originate with us, there is no value to it. Let's be careful not to be puffed up when we get a "God Idea" that brings us prominence or prosperity. But at the same time, let's show some originality. Let's produce something that has our signature to it. Get your own swag, create your own quote, produce your own music and for a change have someone else dance to your music. You have danced long enough to others' music, now it's their turn to dance to yours. Go ahead and start dancing. The words and the music are in you.

WE SHOULD RESPECT AND HONOR
PEOPLE FOR THE OFFICE THEY HOLD,
BUT WE SHOULD BE VERY CAREFUL
THAT WE DO NOT IDOLIZE THEM

CHAPTER
06

Principle #5
CHOOSE HUMILTY OVER
PRIDE AND EGOISM

I have been around in ministry for quite a while and I have seen some very troubling things. It has always bothered me why individuals allow pride to fill their lives, when they already know what the Word states will be the result of pride.

In Luke 14:8-11, Jesus tells us that when we are invited to an event that we should not make ourselves feel overly important. We should not seek the most prominent seats but rather take the lowly seats, lest we cause ourselves to be embarrassed.

I believe that pride and a lack of wisdom usually go together. People who are egoistic and prideful, do not have a relationship with wisdom.

But those of us who are intent on serving our generation cannot allow our egos to get in the way. We must quickly realize that it is not about us but the generation that we are called to serve.

We should have a healthy self-esteem, but it must not take us to the place where we think that we are better than others. Material things such as a beautiful church building, a luxurious home and fancy cars are not true indicators of success. All those things can be taken away in an instant. We must never forget where we came from, and those who helped us along the way. We must pause on many occasions and think back upon our journey through life, and of those who played a pivotal role in helping us to get to where we are today. No man or woman is an island. Taking time to reflect on the roles that others played in helping us, will help us keep our egos in check.

Pieces of the Puzzle

Have you ever heard someone say, "I'm a self-made man"? I hate to disappoint them, but no man or woman is self-made. A few years ago, I decided that for Thanksgiving that year, I was going to feature someone on my Facebook page, each day in the month of November. Every day, I would write something about one person and say why I was thankful for that person. Each of them had played a role in my life to help me in some way large or small. Each of them had contributed to helping me to be where I am today.

When we operate like that, we cannot be egoistic or proud, or feel that we don't owe any one anything for our success. One of my favorite messages that I have shared all over the world, is one that is entitled, "The Piece of the Puzzle".

I was speaking at a conference on the Caribbean island of Barbados, some years ago. In my message, I made an illustration that we are all carrying pieces of the puzzle to other people's lives. I left Barbados and went to fulfil another engagement. When I returned home, I found a Fed Ex envelope addressed to me. Curiously, I opened it and found a letter and a piece of jewelry inside. It was a gold puzzle piece. The letter had been written by a young lady who had attended the conference. She said that she had come to the conference with so many questions that she had been asking of the Lord and that all her questions had been answered. She realized that I had held the piece of the puzzle at that juncture of her life. She had taken some broken pieces of gold to a jeweler and had him fashion it into a gold puzzle piece which she had sent to me to remind me that I am carrying pieces of the puzzle to other people's lives.

I was so touched by her act that I immediately made a change. Prior to this, I always used to wear eagle pendants. I love eagles so much that my South African friends in ministry, had given me the name "Ukhozi", which means "eagle" in the Zulu language. Whenever I would arrive in South Africa, they would say, "The eagle has landed." I love the name and I still love eagles, but I put away my eagle pendants and since that time, I only wear the piece of the puzzle to remind me of my assignment in life, and that I hold pieces of the puzzle for other people's lives.

That young lady thought that I was a blessing to her, but she will never understand the impact that she has had on my life up to this day, after so many years. What she did has helped me to realize that not only am I carrying puzzle pieces for others, but there are those that I am yet to meet who are carrying pieces of the puzzle for my life.as well.

Is it Worth the Risk?

How can I become egoistic and proud and risk turning away those who are destined to play a significant role in my life?

In 2 Corinthians 2:15, the Word of God refers to us as *"a sweet, smelling fragrance, or a pleasant aroma of Christ"*. Humility gives off a sweet aroma. On the contrary, Pride and egoism perverts that fragrance and turns it into a foul odor that repels rather than attracts others. Proud people believe that everything revolves around them. They are motivated by what's in it for them. They want to know who is going to get the credit or what position they will have. Sadly, their friends are either too intimidated to tell them the truth about themselves or are of the same kind of spirit and so never share with them that their behavior is offensive to those around them.

The scriptures warn us several times, about the danger of pride.

Pride goes before destruction and a haughty spirit before a fall
-Proverbs 16:18

When pride comes, then comes disgrace but with humility comes wisdom
-Proverbs 11:2 (NIV)

A person's pride will humble him but a humble spirit will gain honor
-Proverbs 29:23 (HCSB)

If there is anyone who can tell us about how destructive pride can be, it would be Nebuchadnezzar, king of Babylon. He learned his lesson the hard way when he disregarded God's warning to humble himself and ended up insane for seven years. When he came to his senses this is what he said:

"Now I Nebuchadnezzar praise, exult and glorify the King of Heaven because all His works are true and His

ways are just. He is able to humble those who walk in pride".

Daniel 4:37 (HCSB)

We must guard ourselves against the spirit that Diotrephes displayed in the early church. What did Diotrephes do that caused the apostle, John to give him a negative report? He allowed the spirit of pride to get a hold of him and to affect the church.

[9] I wrote to the church, but Diotrephes, who loves to be first, will not welcome us. [10] So when I come, I will call attention to what he is doing, spreading malicious nonsense about us. Not satisfied with that, he even refuses to welcome other believers. He also stops those who want to do so and puts them out of the church.

3 John 9-10 (NIV)

This is what pride will do to us. It will cause us to promote our own self-importance at the expense of others.

"The Important"

Some years ago, I was at a conference for ministers being attended by many ministers from across the country and other parts of the world. A senior pastor of a large church attempted to approach a younger minister from a much smaller church, only to be stopped by a security person from that younger pastor's church. The senior pastor refused to allow himself to be deterred and later recounted the story. I found the incident comical at the least because my thought was, who did that young pastor feel would have wanted to kill him at that conference that necessitated him walking with his security detail?

I'm not denying the importance of a security detail especially in the perilous times in which we now live. When I travel to some countries, they provide us with armed guards because of the threat of kidnappings. It is not something that I request, but a service that the host provides because he deems it necessary.

There are no superstars in the Kingdom. Historically, the Father has used humble people to display His power. Moses, who saw God face to face was described in *Numbers 12:3* as *"very humble, more than all men who were on the face of the earth" (NKJV)*. God made his acts known to Israel but his ways known to Moses. Yet Moses was never egoistic or full of pride.

In Galatians 2:5-6, Paul in his defense of the truth, did not allow those perceived by others to be "the important" people, to have any effect on him.

> *"But we did not give up and submit to these people for even an hour, so that the truth of the gospel would be preserved for you. Now from those recognized as important (what they really were makes no difference to me; God does not show favoritism) they added nothing to me."*

Galatians 2:5-6 (HCSB)

We should respect and honor people for the office they hold, but we should be very careful that we do not idolize them.   The spirit of Hollywood must not influence us. We would all do well to pray David's prayer found in *Psalm 36:11*, *"Let not the foot of pride come against me".* Pride precedes destruction and a haughty spirit will lead to a fall.

DON'T BE DISCOURAGED
ABOUT THOSE WHO
DO NOT LIKE YOU.

CHAPTER
07

Principle #6
DON'T TRY TO GET PEOPLE TO LIKE YOU

Let's face it. Everyone likes to be liked. Don't believe individuals who say, "I don't care whether people like me or not". One of the basic human needs, is the need to be wanted, accepted, loved and even liked.

One of my strongest characteristics, is my love for people. I genuinely love people. I know that the Father has placed a special love in my heart that has enabled me to show that love to people in so many places.

Yet in seeking to serve my generation, I came to realize that not everyone is going to like what I say or how I operate. That has been hard for me to accept because I do not like relationship conflicts and I hate to hurt anyone. But I have learned to embrace what Matthew 18:7 says, *"Woe to the world because of offenses. For offenses must come, but woe to that man by whom the offense comes"* (HSBC)

Unavoidable Offences

As much as we try we cannot avoid offenses. They are a part of life. The only way to avoid offence is to leave this earth and go to heaven where there is no offence. Because, as much as you may try to avoid offending people, people will always take an offence because of you. You can show as much love to people as you can, there will always be those who will never like you or accept you. It does not matter how much you try to love others, it will not be enough.

Sometimes you can tell that someone just does not like you. But if you were to ask them why they do not like you, or what you have done to offend them, they might have a hard time coming up with something.

They have a hard time because they might be unwilling or ashamed to admit the real reason they harbor ill will towards you. I have found that many times individuals who do not like another person may be secretly jealous of that person. They may not admit it, but there is a root of jealousy somewhere. In a previous chapter, we spoke about breaking free from people's unreasonable expectations of you. Well, if we master that, we would be better able to deal with those who do not like us.

You may ask, "But how do I deal with someone that I'm

called to serve but who does not like me?". In a situation like this, my prayer would be to ask God to help me to continue to show them such love that it would melt the hardness that they are displaying towards me. God says in His Word, that if a man's ways please Him, God will cause even his enemies to be at peace with him.

Take Heart, Consider Jesus

It's important to realize that those we are called to serve are not obliged to like us. Take heart from the prophets of old. Most of them were scorned, hated, imprisoned, and even killed, yet they served their generation. Let us consider the example of our Lord Jesus Christ.

No one can claim to love humanity more than Jesus did. **It was love for man that brought Him to earth.** Yet some of the people that He came to serve turned against Him.

Some of those who were singing His praises and laying their garments on the ground for Him, were in the crowd the next day, calling for Him to be crucified.

The Bible tells us that He would not entrust Himself to man when they were praising Him for the miracles He had done because He knew the nature of man.

23 Now when He was in Jerusalem at the Passover, during the feast, many believed in His name when they saw the signs which He did. 24 But Jesus did not commit Himself to them, because He knew all men,

John 2:23-24 (NKJV)

We too, must be always aware of the nature of man. I am not suggesting that we operate with suspicion towards those we serve, but that we bear in mind that we are dealing with man. Remember that no one truly knows the heart of man, but God.

9 "The heart is deceitful above all things,
And desperately wicked;
Who can know it?

Jeremiah 17:9 (NKJV)

We must believe the best about people but do not be blown away if you see or hear something about someone whom you thought could do no wrong. That is why it is important to stay under grace. The Bible tells us that we are kept by the power of God through faith. (1 Peter 1:5)

In my journey of faith, I have always kept my eyes on the Lord. As a young believer growing up, there were moments when I could have allowed myself to become discouraged if I had kept my eyes on men. But I realized that salvation is a personal thing, that I, and no other person was responsible for my personal salvation. I had to work my salvation out for myself. (Philippians 2:12)

When I started out in the ministry after graduating from Bible College, I had moments of great discouragement. I knew that there were those who did not like me, but I had to stay true to my assignment. I had to understand that I could not place too great of an expectation on people. I had to keep my focus on the One who will never betray me but who is always there to help me fulfil my assignment in serving my generation.

In a later chapter we will deal with why some relationships are transient. Have you ever observed people who were so close that nothing seemed to come between them? Yet at some point there was a breakdown in the relationship and a parting of ways. Once inseparable friends, they had now become enemies. It is important to have friends, but always be aware that things can go wrong and that you must guard your heart and not allow yourself to fall apart because of betrayal.

When you have an overwhelming desire to be liked by people, you can find yourself beginning to compromise and giving the impression that you are for sale. I have seen individuals who have worked their way into getting their leader's hearts through giving them gifts. But when the time came for their leaders to correct them, they became resentful towards their leader.

I believe that we can love individuals sincerely and genuinely without turning the control of our assignment over to them. People do not have to like us for us for us to serve them. But wisdom will teach us how to relate to those who don't like us. So, in seeking to relate to difficult people, we must open ourselves up to wisdom. Wisdom will always bring us out victorious.

Don't be discouraged about those who do not like you.

Never expect everyone to applaud you. While you are waiting on the applause of **the few**, you may be neglecting **the many** who are waiting on **_you_** to serve them.

I encourage you to follow Jesus' example of serving people without turning your destiny over to them. Those who are for you are more than those who are against you.

.

YOU ARE HERE TO
CREATE A LASTING AND
SIGNIFICANT IMPACT...

CHAPTER
08

Principle #7

DON'T COMPARE YOURSELF WITH OTHERS

2 Corinthians 10:12

We do not dare to classify or compare ourselves with some who commend themselves. When they measure themselves by themselves and compare themselves with themselves, they are not wise. (NIV)

It is detrimental to our destiny when we start comparing ourselves with others. I know that it's a difficult habit to break, but we must realize and understand that "others" are not the rule and standard by which we should measure ourselves. We can use others as inspiration but when we begin to compare ourselves to them then it can produce unhealthy emotion and mindsets in us.

Cows in a Pasture

I recently read a joke about some cows in a pasture who saw a milk truck go by with the words Homogenized, Pasteurized and Fortified written in large letters. One cow then turned to the others and said, "Makes you feel kind of inadequate doesn't it?"

How many of us can say that we know the full story about the individuals with whom we are comparing ourselves? We may just be seeing the trappings and the "glitter" that they show the world, but we may not know the character of the person. They may have been involved in questionable practices and shady dealings to get to where they are. And if you are a person of the Word, you know that it will not last. Their lack of integrity will eventually expose them. On the other hand, you may not know the trials and the heartache that the person has gone through to be where they are today. Are you able to drink of that cup?

You are not in this business to compete with anyone. **You are here to create a lasting and significant impact** and you cannot do that if your focus is on comparing yourself with others.

What about _____?

There is a very interesting account found in John 21: 20-22. In this narrative, Jesus was restoring Peter and was giving him his assignment. Jesus was dealing only with Peter, He had made no reference to John. But Peter, instead of concentrating on his assignment, wanted to compare his assignment with John's. *"And what shall this man do?"*, he asked Jesus. Jesus basically told Peter that it was none of his business and that he should concentrate on his own assignment.

Isn't it amazing that people spend so much time being critical of others in relation to what they should or should not be doing, when they can better utilize that energy and time making sure that they give attention to their own assignment?

Let's take another look at 2 Corinthians 10:12. Paul said that those who were parading themselves as super apostles were comparing themselves among themselves. He was showing them that they were comparing themselves among their own group. Their standard was their own clan that they had formed.

Therefore, go beyond your own denomination or group and create a higher standard for yourself. Get away from the ideology of smallness. In a forest of shrubs and small trees, the pine tree is king, but in a forest of giant redwood oak trees, it is merely a prince. The Word of God is the giant redwood oak tree. Nothing towers over it. Make His Word your standard and you will never need to compare yourself with others.

Whose Opinion?

I like the way the Bible in Basic English translates 2 Corinthians 10:18, *"For the Lord's approval of a man is not dependent on his opinion of himself, but on the Lord's opinion of him"*. It is good to have a healthy opinion of oneself and we should encourage that practice. But here the Word states that it's not even your opinion that matters, but what the Lord thinks of you. I would like you to know that He thinks highly of you. That is why He chose you.

If we take time to think of the Lord's opinion of us, we would stop trying to compare ourselves with others.

Paul was so sure about his assignment that he did not have the time to be comparing himself with others (Gal.2:6). He respected others. In Galatians 2:2, he acknowledges that Peter's assignment was to be the apostle to the Jews. But Paul was not about comparing his assignment to Peter's. He knew what God had called him to do and he was passionate about it.

It is important to recognize others' assignments but not to the point where we feel intimidated by their success and our own ill-perceived lack of success. Celebrate the success of others. Don't become envious of them but don't look down on yourself and feel that you are not accomplishing much in comparison to them.

God's Assignments are Significant

Have you heard the story about the evangelist who had a one-week revival and was so discouraged by the fact that only one person got converted during that whole revival? He might have been comparing himself with others who had staged successful meetings. What he did not know was that the one person who was saved at his meeting was a little boy named William Graham, whom the world later came to know as Evangelist Billy Graham. Do I need to talk about the impact that this one soul saved has had on the nations of the earth? Look further also and see the impact that Billy Graham's son, Franklin Graham is having through his organization, Samaritan's Purse which has a voice in disaster-torn and war-stricken areas around the world.

Treat every assignment that the Lord has given to you as precious and never think of it as insignificant. Just because you might not have the bright lights and exposure that others have, does not make you less significant than those who do. As I matured in ministry, I learned this, whomever you compare yourself with, can become your intimidator.

I know of situations where leaders have inherited or were placed as heads of organizations or churches and those they now led constantly compared them to their predecessors. The reality is that we cannot escape from this. The danger is when we start to compare ourselves with our predecessor. If the comparison is unflattering to us, it can lead to negative behavior. In some instances, successors, to gain ground, try to make the one they succeeded look bad.

I heard about a situation where a founder of a ministry brought someone else to work with him, with the intention of turning over the ministry to that individual. When that person finally took over, he remarked to the congregation, "Now you all are going to get teaching". What was he doing? He was comparing himself with the one who had given him the opportunity to lead the ministry and was attempting to make himself look good at the expense of making his benefactor look bad. How sad!

Learn as much as you can from others but never fall into the trap of comparing yourself with them.

YOUR REVELATION MUST BE

ANCHORED IN THE
WORD OF GOD.

THAT IS THE REASON PAUL MADE SUCH
A CASE AGAINST THOSE WHO SOUGHT
TO PREACH "ANOTHER GOSPEL"

CHAPTER
09

Principle #8
HAVE TUNNEL VISION

The book of Proverbs is one of my favorite books in the Bible. When I started my journey in the Word of faith, Proverbs chapters 3 and 4 were part of my daily confession for years. It got to the point where I could say them both from memory. Wherever I go, I encourage believers to read a chapter from the book of Proverbs every day. And since there are thirty-one chapters, it's easy to do if you read the chapter that corresponds to the day of the month. It will certainly help to make you wiser.

In Proverbs 4:11, King Solomon is speaking about the path of life and of the importance of keeping God's Word within our hearts. In verse 25 he makes a statement, which in my opinion, is the most powerful expression of what it means to have tunnel vision. Proverbs 4 verse 25 says, *"Let your eyes look forward and fix your gaze straight ahead."* (HCSB)

To have tunnel vision simply means to be focused. Anyone who desires to impact their generation must be focused and remain focused. The challenge is that there is no other period in the history of mankind, when so many distractions constantly bombard us.

What is the first thing you reach for when you wake up in the morning? If you are like me, it's your phone. People today spend more time on their mobile devices than they do watching television or even conversing with others. Those who study relationships are concerned by the fact that family members no longer have time to talk with each other, even when they are together. At the dinner table, one hand holds the phone while the other holds the fork. Social media has us so occupied that there is little time left over to focus on any other activity.

Eyes on the Road!

One of my wife's pet peeves are people who text or read texts while driving. When I'm driving with her, she gets very annoyed if I pick up the phone to see who's texting or messaging me. And she is right to be concerned. The statistics are there to prove that many have lost their lives or caused serious accidents because of texting and driving. So, my wife wants me to stay focused when I'm driving. She wants me to keep my eyes on the road. She reminds me that at the speed at which motorists drive, glancing at a text, is equivalent to crossing an entire football field blindfolded! Not only do you endanger your life, but you put those who are on the journey with you, in harm's way.

Why do jockeys put blinders on their horses? They want to win their race and they don't want their horses to be distracted. They want them to focus on getting to the destination that their riders are taking them.

Competing for our Attention

Solomon, who wrote the book of Proverbs, knew from his own experience how dangerous it is to become distracted. He knew what his assignment from God was, but he became distracted by foreign, idolatrous women, who in his latter days turned his heart away from God.

The morale in this is that there will always be things competing for our attention. Some of these things are not necessarily wrong, but if they serve as distractions, we must identify them and understand that they have come simply to get us off focus.

Some distractions come in the form of people. They mean well but they don't realize that they are being used as distractions to those who want to serve their generation. Some of us find it difficult to say no to people because we have a soft heart. Because I have such a strong desire to help people, I know that I must learn to say no. If I don't, other activities can distract me from what the Lord really wants me to do at that time. If we don't learn to distinguish what we really need to give attention to, we can come to a place in our lives where we will be filled with regret. But if we remain focused, we will be like the apostle Paul. At the end of his life, he could say, *"I have fought a good fight, I have finished my course, I have kept the faith". (1 Timothy 4:7)*

The Young Prophet...

When we lose focus, our vision becomes foggy and obscure. We also start to listen to the wrong voices. We can allow others to lead us in a direction that is contrary to what the Father has laid out for us. We must learn to identify the distractions and make straight paths for our feet. (Hebrews 12:13)

1 Kings 13, relates the account of a young prophet to whom God gave a specific assignment to go to Jeroboam, the King of Israel and pronounce judgment against the altar at Bethel. This young prophet had received his instructions directly from the Lord, Himself. His assignment was clear. He was not to greet anyone or fellowship with anyone on his way to and from his assignment.

The king rejected the prophet's words and was immediately stricken with a withered hand. Then when he begged the young prophet to pray for him, his hand was restored. Because he was grateful, the king invited the prophet to the palace to eat with him and to reward him. But the young prophet refused, citing God's instructions to him not to eat with anyone.

Later, an old prophet who had heard of his response to the king, followed the young prophet and invited him to come and eat with him. To which the young prophet repeated that he could not do that because God had commanded him not to greet anyone or eat with anyone. However, when the old prophet told him that he also was a prophet and that God had spoken to him and that it was okay for him to return with him, the young prophet went to his house and ate.

You would have to read 1 Kings 13 yourself to get all the details of the story. But the end of the story is sad and perplexing. Once the young prophet listened to the older man of God and ate and drank with him, the old prophet delivered a sentence of death upon him because he had disobeyed the Word of the Lord that had come directly to him. As soon as he left the old prophet's home, he was attacked by a lion and killed.

I believe that the young prophet had refused the king's offer because the king represented civil authority. He was an idolatrous king who did not represent God. But the young prophet saw the older prophet as being a representative of God. He listened to him rather than trusting the Word of the Lord that he had received directly from God, Himself. If God had changed His mind, wouldn't He have made it known to Him directly? The young prophet got out of focus by listening to an old "retired" prophet to his own peril. Not having tunnel vision cost him his life.

Stick to It!

We need to know the assignment that the Lord has given to us and learn to stick to it. It is so important for us to know the voice of God. The young prophet should have stuck with what God had said to him instead of what a man was saying to him. Not all prophecies are truly from God, therefore we need a strong sense of discernment to know when it is God and when it is the flesh. You may have heard this humorous story about someone who was prophesying in a church whose prophecy went like this:" Thus sayeth the Lord, do not be afraid my children even though I Myself am afraid sometimes." In that instance we would know that God was not speaking since He is never afraid. But the lesson in this is that not everyone who says, "thus sayeth the Lord is speaking on God's behalf.

We must remember what Paul said in Galatians 1:6-9: that if anyone brings any other gospel to us other than that which we have received, they should be accursed. This is a very strong statement, but we see how important it is when people come up with certain revelations that have no basis in the Word of God.

Sometime ago, someone told me that they had read in a book written by someone who had an out of body experience and went either to Heaven or Hell (I'm not sure which one it was). The person who had that experience, said in the book, that from the time the children of Israel used their jewelry to make a golden calf, God cursed jewelry. I told the individual right away that that was false, that nowhere in the Word of God supports that teaching. I don't care how many people go to Heaven or Hell and come back. If they come with any revelation that has no basis in the Word of God, we do not have to accept it. These things have caused a lot of people to lose their focus and derail their assignment.

Anchored in the Word

Your revelation must be anchored in the Word of God. That was the reason Paul made such a case against those who sought to preach "another gospel".

The job of Satan is to get us side-tracked from our assignment, but we must have tunnel vision and remain focused.

One way that has helped me to keep focused is a daily regimen that I observe. It requires a certain amount of discipline, but I do it because I have learned over the years the importance of the Word of God in our daily lives. So, I begin each day reading about five or six chapters of the Bible from a plan that I follow. Then my wife and I would read aloud from Deuteronomy 28:1-13, Psalm 20:1-9, Psalm 112:1-9, Ephesians 1:17-23 and Ephesians 3:14-20. We personalize these scriptures as we read them and they have helped us to stay in faith as to where the Lord is taking us as we serve our generation.

Another thing that we do daily is the re-affirmation of the covenants that we renew at the beginning of each year. They are the covenants of Life, Health and Healing, Victory, Protection, Grace and Favor and Provision and Abundance. Finally we say out loud our expectations based on Proverbs 23:17 – 18 *"Let not thine heart envy sinners but be thou in the fear of the LORD all the day long. For surely there is an end;*

and thine expectation shall not be cut off."

I believe that every child of God should have expectations and should bring those expectations before Him in the form of daily confessions. If you have no expectations, it could mean that you have lost hope.

Every year I make a new list of expectations that I daily declare before the Lord. Those that are fulfilled we cross out, those that are not yet fulfilled, we carry over to the next year.

These practices have helped me to stay focused. Because of my frequent trips, many times, I do my reading and declarations on the plane if I had a very early flight. Whenever I'm home, my wife and I will do it together or on the way to the airport. Someone may ask, "Isn't that a burden?" No, not when you know the importance of the Word and the joy and upliftment that you get. Is it any wonder that Job said, *"Neither have I gone back from the commandment of his lips; I have esteemed the words of his mouth more than my necessary food". (Job 23:12, KJV)*

Moses stated in Deuteronomy 32:47 *"For it is not an empty or trivial matter for you; indeed it is your [very] life. By [honoring and obeying] this word you will live long in the land, which you are crossing the Jordan to possess." (AMP)*

Experts tell us that it takes just about thirty days to form a habit. Try it for the next thirty days and see whether it helps you to become more focused.

IF YOU ARE WAITING
TO FEEL GOOD TO FORGIVE
AND HAVE A FREE SPIRIT,
YOU WILL HAVE TO WAIT FOR A
VERY LONG TIME FOR THAT
FEELING TO COME.

CHAPTER
10

Principle #9
KEEP YOUR HEART FREE

This principle is the subject of many sermons, but it seems to be the hardest one for believers to practice. As I take the time to delve into this principle and to share some of my experiences, I trust that you will be helped.

Let me start by saying that if we want to affect our generations, we must understand and practice this principle constantly.

Too many leaders are operating from positions of leadership with deep wounds in their hearts. They cannot truly say that their hearts are free because they have not gone past their hurts. In the quest to have our hearts free, there are some basic things that we need to understand.

Nothing to do with Your Feelings

If you are waiting to feel good to forgive and have a free spirit, then you will have to wait for a very long time for that feeling to come.

Forgiveness is from the spirit. Your emotions will fall in line after you have dealt with forgiving the person or persons from the spirit (heart).

In Matthew 18:35, Jesus tells us that forgiveness is from the heart. What is the heart? It is the spirit of man. We have been tormenting ourselves trying to forgive people from our soul (emotions, mind). However, it is with our spirit that we must purpose or determine that we are going to forgive. When your emotions want to rise up, then from your spirit, which is the real you, you speak to your soul (the place where your emotions reside) and tell it that the matter has already been dealt with and that it no longer has any hold on you. Then each day you confess that your heart is free from offences. I hope this is helping you because I know that no one reading this book can say that they have never offended someone or been offended by someone, unless you don't live in this world. This leads me to my second point.

No Matter How Hard You Try... It Will Happen

It does not matter how hard you try not to offend, or be offended, it will happen. Luke 17:1 says that *it is impossible but that offences will come....(KJV)* The only way to avoid offences is to go to heaven. That is the only place where there are no offences. I tend to believe that there are also offences in hell.

We must make room for offences. I am not insinuating in any way that you should go out looking for someone to offend you, but that we should be prepared to handle offences whenever they come, because they will come.

How we deal with offences is entirely up to each one of us. It has nothing to do with the person who caused the offence, because our ability or willingness to forgive them is not dependent on their behavior or attitude. Stop putting pressure on yourself by trying to dictate the offender's behavior. We are only in control of our response to their behavior, we have no control whatsoever over their behavior.

The Lord has taught me many lessons in that area. Why do believers struggle so much in this area? It is because of the flesh. The flesh always seeks justification. That is why we go to great lengths to exempt ourselves from any wrong doing when we have offended someone. We even go as far as to accuse the offended person of over-reacting or misconstruing our actions.

Here's the rule by which I operate. If someone tells me that I offended him, I do not try to justify myself because I am not the one who is offended. It's not my feelings that are in question, it is the other person's. My only recourse is to genuinely say to that person that I am sorry that I offended him or her. Too many times we expect others to operate at our perceived level of maturity and we are impatient with them for having taken an offence.

Apologizing vs. Forgiving

Has it ever occurred to you that the word, "apologize" is not a biblical word? That word has crept into the Christian vocabulary seemingly to replace the term "to ask for forgiveness". What's the difference you might ask? There is a great difference.

"Apologize" is a secular word that is used to replace "to ask for forgiveness". How often do we hear of individuals in the secular world, who have inflicted pain or caused hurt to individuals or groups, being called upon to ask for forgiveness? I've never heard of it. Rather, when political or social pressure is brought to bear upon them, they may issue a statement of apology for their actions or words. Does that mean that their heart is changed? Not necessarily. You can apologize without being sorry, but you cannot ask for forgiveness without being genuinely sorry.

So, the word "apologize" is not one that I use. If I have

caused hurt or pain, then I genuinely repent by saying, "I'm sorry, please forgive me".

The "IF" of Offence

One of the things that bother me when I am acting as a mediator, is the phrase, "*if* I have offended you". Any time someone starts off by saying "if", I stop them right away. I tell them that it's not a matter of "if", the other person is offended but is willing to be reconciled. But when you preface your repentance with the phrase "If I have offended you", you are refusing to validate the other person's sense of hurt or betrayal. You are minimizing how they feel and you are really saying that you don't believe that you offended them. As I said earlier, in cases of offence, it is the offended person's feelings that matter, not the feelings of the one who did the offending.

The next time someone tells you that you offended them, please don't use the word "if" when asking for forgiveness. Your flesh might rebel against it, but your spirit will rejoice when you say from the heart, "I'm deeply sorry for the pain I caused you, will you please forgive me."

Forgiveness... Not For Their Benefit

It is dangerous to hold on to un-forgiveness. When we do so, we are hurting ourselves more than the one we refuse to forgive. It is equivalent to drinking poison and expecting the other person to die.

Do you know anyone who is holding a grudge against someone else, to the point where even their health is affected? Do you know that in most cases like that, the unforgiven person has gone on with life, blissfully unaware that the person holding the grudge is still mad at them?

When we forgive those who have offended us, **we are the greatest beneficiary of the forgiveness we have extended.**

Our spirit feels light and our body and soul are protected from the by- products of the unhealthy emotions such as anger, resentment and bitterness that accompany unforgiveness. These emotions are the fuel for certain diseases in the body. In Hebrews 12:15, the Word of God admonishes us to be careful not to allow any root of bitterness in our heart to spring up and defile us. Always remember, **you are not responsible for another person's behavior, you are only responsible for how you choose to respond to their actions.**

The Bible Does Not Say to Forgive & Forget

Many believers live with condemnation because they have been told that the Bible says to forgive and forget. Therefore, when they remember the hurt that they experienced, they start to doubt that they have really forgiven their offender.

I have good news for you. Just because the thought of what was done to you comes back to you, it does not mean that you are walking in unforgiveness.

The children of Israel suffered terrible injustice at the hands of the Egyptians. Yet when God delivered them, He told them NOT TO FORGET what they had gone through in Egypt. Why? Because God did not want them to treat strangers and foreigners the way that the Egyptians had treated them. (Exodus 22:21, Exodus 23:9, Deuteronomy 10:19) In fact, God constantly reminded them of how they were treated and commanded them to be kind to strangers and foreigners.

The hurt you experienced may never be totally erased from your memory, so don't condemn yourself if the memory surfaces. Instead use it to resolve that you will not inflict that same hurt upon someone else. That is what God wanted the children of Israel to do with the memory of their pain, and that is what He wants us to do also.

Forgiveness Empowers

Offences should never destroy or weaken you. They should build character in you. If your hurts leave you bitter, then it means that you have not learned anything from your experiences. You become stronger in character when you learn to keep your heart free. You must become better and not bitter.

You have not truly forgiven if every time you see the person who offended you, you pass another way to avoid them. If you begin to feel awkward around them, remind yourself that you decided from your heart to forgive them and therefore they do not have any power over you or your emotions any more. If you constantly practice that, you will soon discover that you have a free heart and that is a very wonderful thing to experience.

A free heart is absolutely necessary for the love of God and the Holy Spirit to flow unhindered in our lives as we seek to serve our generation.

INSTEAD OF REJOICING IN THE SUCCESSES OF OUR SONS AND DAUGHTERS, TOO MANY TIMES, FATHERS OR MENTORS BECOME INTIMIDATED.

CHAPTER 11

Principle #10
DO NOT BE INTIMIDATED BY THE SUCCESS OF THOSE YOU HAVE RAISED UP

What is Jesus' desire for the church? Isn't is that we should do greater works than He did? As His Body, when we do greater works, we make Him "look good". This same desire should be in the heart of every leader and mentor. We are called to raise up sons and daughters, who will do greater works than we have done.

Unfortunately, instead of rejoicing in the successes of our sons and daughters, too many times, fathers or mentors become intimidated.

If we are not careful, a jealous spirit can take a hold of us and make us become like King Saul instead of Barnabas.

Saul, in a sense was David's mentor. However, instead of rejoicing at David's success as a warrior, Saul became jealous because the women attributed thousands to him and tens of thousands to David. Saul became so intimidated and jealous that he actively sought to kill David.

If we find ourselves wanting our sons and daughters to fail because we feel they are trying to eclipse us, we need a serious heart checkup. We must rid ourselves of that spirit of Saul that manifests itself in wishing for the downfall of those who are serving us.

The One Who Mentored Paul

We must foster the spirit of Barnabas who was Paul's (Saul's) elder in the faith. Barnabas was the one who mentored Paul during the early years of his conversion. We usually think of the Apostle Paul as a giant of the faith, but we tend to forget that it was Barnabas who mentored him. That is why the book of Acts refers to Barnabas and Saul during those early days of his ministry. When Paul's assignment to the church became clear and his influence began to increase, Barnabas very graciously relinquished the leadership to Paul. From that time on, Acts began to refer to the team as Paul and Barnabas.

The name Barnabas, means "son of consolation, or son of encouragement". He understood his assignment in life. His primary role in life was to be a voice for those who seemed to have no voice. When none of the apostles believed that he was genuinely converted, Barnabas became a voice for Saul (Paul) and vouched for him. Barnabas went even further and left a great revival to go and find Saul and take him under his wings. Do you realize that even though Paul says that the revelation he received was not from man but from God, that he still needed that human touch in his life to mentor him?

Parting Ways...

In Acts 15:35 - 40, we read the account of a strong disagreement between Paul and Barnabas which eventually led them to part ways. John Mark wanted to go with Paul and Barnabas on their second missionary trip. But Paul adamantly refused to accept him because he had deserted them on the first missionary journey. Barnabas wanted to give the young man a second chance, but Paul refused. Barnabas was infuriated because he knew that when no one believed in

Paul, he was the one who stood up for him. Now Paul was not willing to extend that same mercy to John Mark.

Because of his assignment to be a voice, an encourager and an advocate for those who needed a second chance, Barnabas put his relationship with Paul on the line and refused to back down. His assignment to Paul was over, his assignment to John Mark had begun. Did he make the right decision? He obviously did. Many years later, when the Apostle Paul was in a cold Roman prison and deserted by many of those he had trusted, he wrote to Timothy and asked him to bring John Mark with him because he was "profitable" or useful to him for ministry (2 Tim. 4:11). This was the one that Paul had rejected because of his earlier failure, but who had become profitable in the years that followed, because someone (Barnabas) believed in him.

Remaining True

As important a lesson as this serves to us, my emphasis is not on John Mark's success, but on the character of Barnabas who stuck to his assignment and stood up for John Mark as he had stood up for Paul. Even though Paul had begun to supersede him as an apostle, he did not become jealous of Paul, neither did he allow himself to be intimidated by Paul's prominence. Instead, just as Paul had publicly withstood Peter and Barnabas for their hypocrisy when they stopped eating with the Gentiles when some of the Jewish apostles were there, so too Barnabas remained true to his assignment.

We should not ever allow ourselves to feel that we cannot reprove someone we mentored because they now have a place of preeminence. If we see that person operating contrary to clearly defined principles of the Word, we are responsible to warn him.

Part of my assignment is to be a "connector" in the Kingdom of God. Through the conferences that our ministry hosts, we have been able to expose to the Body of Christ, apostles, prophets, teachers, pastors and evangelists, who are not well known, but who are tremendously gifted and operate under a heavy anointing. Some of them had been ministering faithfully in "the backside of the desert", and our ministry was blessed to be able to bring their gifts to the attention of other men and women of God. Many of them have gone on to surpass me. Am I jealous of them? Absolutely not! It gives me great joy that I had a part to play in giving them the opportunity to connect to others who were able to take them even further than I could.

We should count it as an honor and privilege that the Father should entrust us with the destinies of His children, by allowing us to be there for them at whatever stage of the journey we were needed. We have even more to be thankful for, if we have helped them to discover their assignment so that they can properly serve their generation.

IF WE PROPERLY UNDERSTAND
STEWARDSHIP, WE WILL REALIZE THAT
IT IS THE FATHER'S GREAT PLEASURE
TO GIVE US MORE TO MANAGE.

WHEN HE FINDS US TRUSTWORTHY,
HE WILL PUT INTO OUR HANDS AN
ABUNDANCE OF WEALTH
TO MANAGE
FOR THE WORK OF THE KINGDOM.

CHAPTER 12

Principle #11
USE YOUR RESOURCES
TO SERVE YOUR GENERATION

We need to have a proper understanding of wealth if we are going to serve our generation. We must view wealth from a Kingdom perspective and not from the perspective of the world. The Bible refers to us as stewards. The word means, among other definitions, "a manager or one who is put in charge of that which belongs to another. From that perspective, we don't own anything. All that we seem to have, really belongs to the Lord. This includes not just our material possessions, but also those relationships that we treasure the most.

When we understand this principle, we will not hold on tightly to our material possessions. There is enough money and resources in the Kingdom to publish the news of the King in every corner of the earth. But the citizens of the Kingdom have not understood that they are stewards of the King and so, many of them have a hard time giving to the cause of the King because they think that whatever money or resources they have is theirs.

If we properly understand stewardship, we will realize that it is the Father's great pleasure to give us more to manage. When He finds us trustworthy, He will put into our hands an abundance of wealth to manage for the work of the Kingdom. **He does not have a problem with us having things, He has a problem with things having us.**

What would your answer be if you were to ask yourself the question, "How much of my resources have I committed to serving my generation? You may be a tither. You give ten percent of your income. But until you are willing to go beyond the tithe, which is really just the Kingdom tax, and to ask yourself, "How much should I keep?", you have not grasped the essence of what it means to be a steward.

A Common Challenge

One of the areas that many believers face the greatest challenge is in giving. We have been told that only about five percent of Christians in America are faithful tithers. Yet we have accomplished so much with five percent. Can you imagine the kind of impact that the Church can have globally if only fifty percent would become faithful tithers?

If a believer struggles with the practice of tithing, then

we can be very sure that he will not be able to be a generous giver. I will go even further to say that just because a believer gives tithes does not qualify him to be considered a giver. Tithing is elementary. It's a Kingdom tax that we owe to God for the use of His facilities and resources that He has made available to us. You become a giver when you learn to go over and above the tithe and begin to sow. There is a difference between a tither and a sower.

A tither is someone who gives the ten percent and no more.

The tither operates from his comfort zone. But **the sower is one who steps out from his comfort zone** and with sweat, tears and pain, **chooses to become partners with God to accomplish His will on the earth.**

An individual like this has the sure promises of God that

though they "sow in tears", they shall surely "reap in joy". (Psalm 126:6, Hebrews 6:10)

Anyone who is not a consistent tither will never be a consistent sower. The first step to becoming a sower is to become a faithful tither. Once we master the practice of tithing, we put ourselves in the position to become a sower. In other words, we graduate from the elementary stage of tithing in order to become a sower.

Warrior... Worshipper... Giver

One of the most powerful examples of stewardship that I have found in the Scriptures, is that of David. David served his generation by the will of God, and then then died. Most people know of David as a mighty warrior. Some know him to be a great worshipper. But David was also a giver. He used his resources to serve his generation and through his giving, he influenced and affected his generation in a great way.

When David contributed from his private funds to the building of the tabernacle, it is recorded that part of his contribution was three thousand talents of gold.

1 Chronicles 29:3-4

"I now give my personal treasures of gold and silver for the temple of my God, over and above everything I have provided for this holy temple: three thousand talents of gold and seven thousand talents of silver..." (NIV)

A talent weighed seventy- five pounds. If we were to value that in today's currency, David's contribution amounted to over a trillion dollars. Then verse 9 tells us that David the King rejoiced greatly.

David had no problem in giving his resources to serve his generation because **he understood where his wealth had come from and that he was merely a steward.**

In chapter 29 of 1 Chronicles, David repeatedly alludes to the fact that all that he and his people had, came from God. (1 Chronicles 29:11, 12, 14, 16) In verse 18, he prays and asks God to forever keep the knowledge of the fact that they were stewards before them.

"Kingdom Paymasters"

We must have faith to know that when we use our resources to serve our generation, God, our Father will surely come through for us.

What encourages me in my sowing is the fact that God cannot lie and that He is no man's debtor. He will not allow us to reproach Him. He said in Romans 13:8, that *we should owe no man anything except love*. Since He said that to us, how can He, Himself owe us after we have given to Him? We can paraphrase Ephesians 6:8, to say that what we make happen for others, He will make happen for us.

I always look for opportunities to sow. We must cultivate the spirit of sowing and ask God to make us paymasters in His Kingdom. If you give yourself to Him to become a paymaster, then He will give you the seed to sow. A paymaster is one who has committed himself to respond whenever a need is presented. A paymaster is usually one of the first to support, to pledge, and to give. Paymasters are financiers in the Kingdom. Because God gives bread to some individual and seed to others.

Paymasters will never lack because they are sowers, and God continuously gives seed to the sower.

My prayer is that you will be willing to use your resources to finance the Father's program by becoming a paymaster, and by so doing, serve your generation.

GOD HAS SUCH A
STRONG DESIRE
FOR US TO SUCCEED IN LIFE,
THAT ALL ALONG THE PATH TO OUR
DESTINY, AT STRATEGIC POINTS,
HE PLACES INDIVIDUALS WITH

PIECES OF THE PUZZLE
TO OUR LIVES TO HELP US TO ACHIEVE
OUR PURPOSE

CHAPTER 13

Principle #12
UNDERSTAND THAT NOT ALL
RELATIONSHIPS ARE PERMANENT

If we want to understand the role that assignments play in our lives, we must learn quickly that all relationships are not designed to be permanent. Too many individuals are carrying scars from broken relationships because they held on to certain relationships past their season.

Let me make a disclaimer right at the very beginning. When I say that not all relationships are meant to be permanent, I am in no way referring to the marriage relationship. So please do not use what I am about to say as a justification to put away your spouse.

The Jigsaw Puzzle

Our lives are basically made up of seasons and assignments. God has such a strong desire for us to succeed in life, that all along the path to our destiny, at strategic points, He places individuals with pieces of the puzzle to our lives to help us to achieve our purpose.

This is how I usually explain it. Our lives are like a completed jigsaw puzzle. At the point at which we are born again, God, the Father takes us from this beginning and shows us the completed picture of our destiny. But He never shows us what lies between the beginning and the end. He then dismantles the picture, takes us back to the beginning and commissions us to make our way to the complete picture that He has shown us.

Every child of God knows the beginning AND the end because the Word of God clearly reveals that we win. But what we don't know, is what we will have to go through on our way to our destiny. That is why I did not say the beginning TO the end, because that is not revealed to us. However, along the path certain people show up with pieces of the puzzle, that are necessary if we are to successfully serve our generation. Likewise, we also carry pieces of the puzzle for others along the way.

However, when these persons turn up either to hand us a piece of the puzzle or for us to give them a piece, we must realize that in most cases, it is for a season. Have you met Christians who appear to be stagnant? Sometimes it is because they are holding on to the people God sent into their lives thinking that those people have come into their lives to stay. In fact, their assignment may have been to just deliver the piece and move on.

We, in turn, must not allow individuals to whom we have been sent for a season to latch unto to us and prevent us from moving on to others who are waiting for us on the journey of their lives. We need to have a broader concept of this vision that we are all carrying pieces of the puzzle to the lives of others. Many of them cannot be complete without us.

I am sure that many of us can remember people who came into our lives at a very crucial and critical moment. Where are those people now? As much as you would have loved to hold on to them, both you and they have moved on. Sometimes God, Himself, had to allow a break up in the relationship because we wanted to "pitch a tent" there and camp at that juncture of our lives.

God's purpose for our lives is of such paramount importance that He will not allow us to "pitch tent". We are, in fact, pilgrims on an ever moving, ever shifting journey.

When The Assignment is Over...

I enjoy meeting new people. I like making new friends. But I realize that not all those friends are going to be in my life on a permanent basis. As I reflect upon my life, I think of the myriads of people that the Lord brought into my life and who impacted my life greatly because they carried major pieces of the puzzle. Where are they today? Did something happen to separate us? No. Their assignment was over. Some of them I would like to contact so that we can get back together, but it may never happen. As much as I have fond memories of these relationships and even a great love and gratitude for them, I had to realize that all relationships are not meant to be permanent.

I can almost hear you asking, "How do I know when an assignment is over?" Here are some signs:

1. *You have lost your joy in each other's company. You pretend to be excited, but you cannot pretend all the time.*

2. *You tolerate the person, or you get the impression that the person is only tolerating you. And by now you have probably heard the saying, "go where you are celebrated not where you are tolerated".*

3. *The other person or perhaps you, take days to return calls or text, even though you are getting each other's messages.*

4. *You are making excuses as to why you can't meet up for events that you never would have missed before.*

But how do you extricate yourself from such a relationship without hurting the other person's feelings? This is just one more of those occasions where the Word of God admonishes us to "acknowledge Him in all of our ways" Proverbs 3:5. We can ask the Lord to cause a smooth and gentle drift away on both sides and He will do it.

However, there are some occasions, if you are the one in the mentoring position, you will have to lovingly, but firmly, release the other person.

If you are the mentee in the relationship, you will have to handle this with much prayer and wisdom. In the mentor-mentee relationship, it is the mentor who should be the one to do the releasing. However, if you find yourself in the position where you truly know by the leading of the Lord that it is the end of a season, but your mentor continues to hold unto you, you will have to respectfully share with your mentor that you appreciate all that he has done for you, but you know that it is time for you to come out from under his wings so that you can fulfill your own destiny and assignment. Be very careful in doing this that you do not cause your mentor any harm. Learn from the example of David, who refused to harm King Saul even when he was in the position to do so. Remember that your mentor is still the Lord's anointed and that God is looking to see how you treat that covenant relationship.

As we come to the end of this book, know that you are important to the Father's plan for humanity. Don't sit around waiting for someone to show up with a piece of the puzzle for you. Look at your hands. What do you see? You too are carrying pieces of the puzzle to the lives of so many others. As you become aware of this and seek to fulfil this assignment, you will be among those who serve their generation through understanding assignment.

ABOUT THE AUTHOR

Ashley C. Estrada is the Founder and President of Kingdom Life International Christian Center, on the beautiful island of St. Thomas, US Virgin Islands and Kissimmee, Florida. In addition to having been a pastor for over 30 years, Apostle Estrada has served as a father to many pastors and ministers. In this capacity, God has used him to be an avenue for causing divine connections to take place. Many have been given the opportunity to travel with Apostle Estrada on missionary trips to various parts of the world.

The apostolic aspect of the vision of Apostle Estrada's is the birthing of churches in various states and countries of the world. His organization, Ashley Estrada Ministries, exists to provide the whole counsel of God to all who will receive it. His vision to spread God's Word around the world has taken him to Japan more than 40 times, where he is assisting pastors, giving guidance and as a result many churches experience growth. He has also ministered in several parts of the United States, Great Britain, the Philippines, Nigeria, South Africa, Albania, India and the Ukraine, as well as several countries throughout the Caribbean.

Apostle Estrada resides in Kissimmee Florida with his wife Marcia and is the proud father of Joel, Kenneth, Kristel, Jesse, and Jeriah and the grandfather of Ja'el, Kezia, Ethan, Kenneth Mark Cole, and Isaak.

www.ashleyestradaministries.com

Made in the USA
Columbia, SC
05 July 2018